Crystals

by Melissa Stewart

Heinemann Library
CHICAGO, ILLINOIS

Designed by Ox and Company

An Editorial Directions book

Printed in Hong Kong

06 05 04 03 02
10 9 8 7 6 5 4 3 2

Library of Congress Cataloging-in-Publication Data
Stewart, Melissa.
   Crystals / Melissa Stewart.
     p. cm.—(Rocks and minerals)
Includes bibliographical references and index.
Summary: Provides an overview of crystals including their structure and
composition, history, significance, and uses throughout the world.
   ISBN: 1-58810-254-8 (HC), 1-4034-0090-3 (Pbk.)
   1. Minerals—Juvenile literature. 2. Crystals—Juvenile literature. [1. Minerals.
   2. Crystals. 3. Crystallography.] I. Title.
   QE365.2 .S74 2002
   549'.18—dc21   2001002755

Acknowledgments
The author and publishers are grateful to the following for permission to reproduce copyright material:

Photographs ©: Cover background, Brian Parker/Tom Stack & Associates; cover foreground, Mark A. Schneider/Visuals
Unlimited, Inc.; p. 4, Gamma Liaison/Hulton/Archive; p. 5 Jose Manuel Sanchis Calvete/Corbis; p. 6 Tom & Therisa
Stack/Tom Stack & Associates; p.7 S.K. Mittwede/Visuals Unlimited, Inc.; p. 8 Roberto de Gugliemo/Science Photo
Library/Photo Researchers, Inc.; pp. 9, 10 Mark A. Schneider/Visuals Unlimited, Inc.; p. 11 Ken Lucas/Visuals Unlimited, Inc.;
p. 13, Joe Carini/The Image Works; p. 14 Jeff J. Daly/Visuals Unlimited, Inc.; p. 15 Gary Milburn/Tom Stack & Associates; p.
16 Prism Rogers/Martin/FPG International; p. 17 Ken Lucas/Visuals Unlimited, Inc.; p. 18 top A.J. Copley/Visuals Unlimited,
Inc.; p. 18 bottom Arthur Hill/Visuals Unlimited, Inc.; p. 19 Grace Davies Photography; p. 20 Cameramann International,
Ltd.; p. 21 Volker Steger/Science Photo Library/Photo Researchers, Inc.; p. 22 Allen B. Smith/Tom Stack & Associates; p. 23
Ken Lucas/Visuals Unlimited, Inc.; p. 24 William J. Weber/Visuals Unlimited, Inc.;
p. 25 Cabisco/Visuals Unlimited, Inc.; p. 26 Allen B. Smith/Tom Stack & Associates; pp. 27, 28, 29 A.J. Copley/Visuals
Unlimited, Inc.

Some words are shown in bold, **like this.** You can find out what they mean by looking in the glossary.

Contents

What Is a Crystal?

What does a sparkling diamond have in common with a snowflake and the salt you sprinkle on your french fries? They are all crystals. A crystal is a natural solid made of **atoms** that are always arranged in the same way. If no outside forces act on a crystal as it forms, it will have a regular shape and smooth, flat sides called **faces.**

Some crystals contain only one kind of atom. For example, a diamond is made entirely of carbon atoms. Most crystals contain two or more kinds of atoms. Crystals of table salt are made of sodium and chlorine atoms. Ice crystals, or snowflakes, are made of hydrogen and oxygen atoms.

This jewelry features many stunning diamond crystals and one very large sapphire crystal. Diamond contains only carbon atoms, while sapphire contains aluminum and oxygen atoms with a little bit of iron or titanium mixed in.

Crystals are formed when the **minerals** in molten rock gradually become solid. The diamonds, sapphires, and rubies you see in rings and necklaces

WHAT A DISCOVERY!

In 1772, a French scientist named Rome de l'Isle figured out that the atoms inside a crystal are arranged in units that stack together in a regular way.

are all examples of big, beautiful crystals. Not all minerals form crystals the size of the diamonds you see in jewelry. The crystals that make up the minerals feldspar and chalcedony are usually very small.

Minerals join together to form rocks. Some rocks are made of just one kind of mineral, but most contain from two to ten minerals. Slate is a rock that is sometimes used to build floor tiles or beautiful walkways. It usually contains the minerals mica, quartz, and pyrite. Each of these minerals is made up of crystals. Crystals of pyrite contain iron and sulfur atoms.

DID YOU KNOW?

Pyrite is not the only mineral that contains iron and sulfur. Chalcopyrite (left) is made up of iron, sulfur, and copper atoms. People often mine chalcopyrite and heat it to remove the copper crystals. Then they use the copper to make pipes that carry water or wires that conduct electricity.

Seven Kinds of Crystals

You probably see table salt every day, but have you ever looked at it really closely? If you did, you would see that each tiny crystal of salt is shaped like a cube, which has six **faces.** Crystals of the **minerals** galena, fluorite, and pyrite also have six faces.

Not all crystals are shaped like cubes. If you look at a calcite crystal, you will see that it looks different from a crystal of salt. A calcite crystal has eight faces, instead of six. Crystals of ice and graphite also have eight faces. Most crystals have one of seven different shapes. A crystal's shape and the location of its faces can help scientists to identify it.

DID YOU KNOW?

Hundreds of years ago, table salt was as valuable as gold is today. In some parts of Europe and Asia, people used salt to buy and sell things just as we use money today. Why was salt worth so much? In the days before refrigerators existed, salt was needed to dry out meat and some other foods to preserve them for future use.

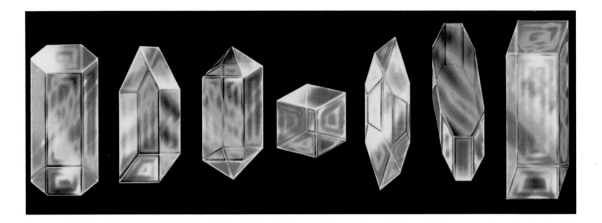

Scientists who study crystals are called **crystallographers.** A Danish physician named Nicolaus Steno may have been the world's first crystallographer. Today, crystallographers have a special way of "seeing" what a crystal's inner structure looks like. They use high-powered electron microscopes to photograph the shadows and reflections of the crystal's **atoms.** Crystallographers can then use this information to figure out how the atoms are arranged.

Nearly all crystals have one of these seven shapes.

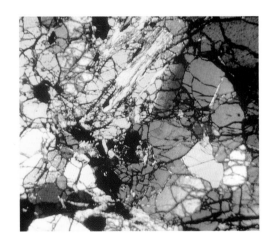

This is what an olivine crystal looks like through an electron microscope. Light microscopes can magnify objects up to 2,000 times, but an electron microscope can magnify objects as much as 1,000,000 times.

SEE FOR YOURSELF

It may seem hard to believe, but even though every ice crystal has six faces, no two snowflakes are identical. Each one is a little different from the rest. To see this for yourself, put a piece of black construction paper in the freezer and wait for the next snowstorm. Catch some snowflakes on the black paper and look at each one with a hand lens.

It's a Habit

A habit is something you do regularly. Some people have a habit of saying certain words, such as "Cool!" or "Awesome!" Other people have a habit of chewing gum.

Believe it or not, crystals have habits too. When a **mineral** has enough raw materials and plenty of room to grow, it forms a large, beautiful crystal. Then the crystal's habit—its shape on the outside—has the same regular, repeating pattern as the **atoms** inside it.

Outside forces, such as heat or pressure, sometimes prevent a crystal from developing normally. Then its habit may look more like a blossoming flower,

DID YOU KNOW?

If a tiny piece of rock or another material lands on a crystal as it is forming, the crystal may be affected. Sometimes you have to look at the crystal through a microscope to see the difference. In other cases, the particle can make a very big difference. When brownish-yellow, needlelike crystals of titanium oxide form inside a crystal of quartz, the result is called "maiden hair" (right).

In 1666, Mount Vesuvius—a **volcano** in Italy—erupted without warning. When people saw rock crosses falling from the sky, they thought God was telling them they would be safe. But those "crosses" weren't really signs from God. They were twinned crystals of pyroxene that were blasted out of the ground and then fell back to Earth.

a religious cross, or even a blob. Gypsum often forms beautiful crystals, but under some conditions it has a flower-shaped habit called "desert rose." Sometimes one crystal grows against or through another crystal in a process called **twinning.** Staurolite, aragonite, and pyroxene all can form twins. Some twinned crystals have alternating colors.

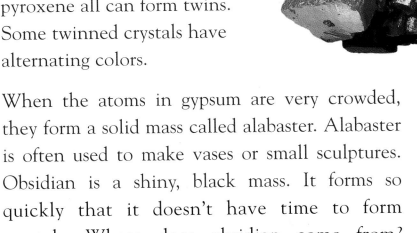

Crystals of aragonite are often long and brittle. Sometimes they intersect and grow together, forming a cross-shaped structure.

When the atoms in gypsum are very crowded, they form a solid mass called alabaster. Alabaster is often used to make vases or small sculptures. Obsidian is a shiny, black mass. It forms so quickly that it doesn't have time to form crystals. Where does obsidian come from? It is made of lava that cools and hardens when it contacts air or water.

Crystals Can Form in Water

Such large, beautiful crystals are very rare. They form only in places that go undisturbed for long periods of time.

When materials dissolved in a liquid such as water join together and form a solid material, **mineral** crystals often grow. The **atoms** may join because the water cools down or because some of the water **evaporates.**

Large crystals of the mineral calcite often form near hot springs. Other kinds of quartz may also form as warm waters cool. Crystals of the minerals galena, fluorite, and barite form when hot waters flow through rock deep below Earth's surface.

The beautiful travertine crystals that make up stalactites form when water drips from the ceiling of a cave and then evaporates, leaving behind a tiny deposit.

IMAGINE THAT!

Have you ever noticed a hard white material slowly building up inside a tea kettle? That material is made up of mineral crystals left behind when water evaporated to form steam.

Over time, the crystals slowly build up. The stalagmites that grow up from the floor of a cave form in the same way. Other beautiful structures found in caves form as crystals of calcite and gypsum slowly build up over time.

The crystals of two minerals we use every day formed millions of years ago when ancient seas and lakes dried up. Today, salt is mined from land that was once covered by salty seas. Crystals of borax formed as the water in ancient lakes slowly evaporated. Today, we use borax to keep our clothes clean and bright and to make heavy, durable glass that can be used to bake breads, cakes, and pies.

Borax crystals contain atoms of boron, sodium, and oxygen. Natural borax deposits are found in California, Chile, Germany, and Italy.

Crystals Can Form in Magma

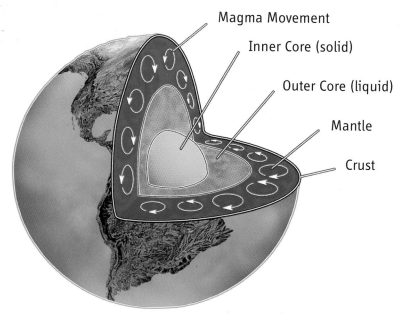

Magma Movement
Inner Core (solid)
Outer Core (liquid)
Mantle
Crust

The thin outer layer of Earth is the crust. The next layer, the mantle, is made of magma that is constantly moving. The core is made of an outer liquid core and an inner solid core.

Below Earth's thin **crust** is an 1,800-mile (2,900-kilometer)-thick layer called the **mantle.** The mantle is made of hot, liquid rock called **magma.** At Earth's center is a sizzling hot **core.** Some parts of that core are hotter than the surface of the Sun.

Heat energy from the core is always escaping into the mantle. All that energy forces molten magma to churn constantly within the mantle. Once in a while, magma finds a crack in Earth's crust and travels all the way to the surface to spill onto the land through a **volcano.** Then the hot, flowing material is called lava. As the lava quickly cools, tiny crystals of the minerals feldspar, pyroxene, and olivine grow and form basalt, phonolite, andesite, and other kinds of **igneous rock.**

Not all escaping magma makes it to Earth's surface, however. Some gets trapped at the top of the mantle or within the crust. This magma cools much more slowly than lava and forms larger crystals. Beautiful crystals of tourmaline, diamond, topaz, sapphire, and ruby grow slowly over thousands—or even millions—of years.

These valuable crystals come to Earth's surface only when all the surrounding igneous rock is slowly broken down and worn away. At the same time that magma is cooling to create new igneous rock, other forces on Earth's surface are working to destroy existing rock. Over time, wind and water can **erode** even the toughest rock. Rocks can also be broken down by creatures in the soil, by plant roots, and by repeated freezing and thawing. This is called **weathering.**

Because many of the most valuable crystals are very hard, they can stand up to erosion and weathering. That is why sapphires, rubies, diamonds, and emeralds are often found in the sandy material that forms on riverbeds or in gravel left behind when a stream or river changes its course.

After lava explodes out of a volcano, such as Kilauea on the island of Hawaii, it cools and hardens to form igneous rock. Because air cools lava quickly, volcanic rock usually contains very small crystals.

Gems and Gemstones

A **gemstone** is a mineral that has large, beautiful crystals and is durable enough to wear as jewelry. After a gemstone is cut and polished, it is called a **gem** or a jewel.

Topaz, tourmaline, garnet, alexandrite, and peridot are all beautiful and durable gemstones. They are called "semiprecious" because they are fairly common and relatively inexpensive.

Sapphires, rubies, and emeralds are all precious gemstones. They are rare, so they cost a lot of money. Diamonds are the most prized gemstones of all. Diamond is the hardest mineral on Earth, and it sparkles with a fiery brilliance.

Danburite, tanzanite, blende, and sphene are all minerals with beautiful crystals, but they are not gemstones. They are soft and scratch easily, so they are rarely made into jewelry.

Gemstones are beautiful, but gems look even better. That's because gem cutters know a few tricks. Over

The value of a cut gemstone is based on its beauty, rarity, hardness, and how it has been cut and polished. A gem cutter will choose a shape to best display the unique qualities of the stone.

DID YOU KNOW?

Gems are measured in carats. The word "carat" comes from a Greek word meaning "carob bean." One carat weighs about 0.007 ounces (0.2 grams)—about as much as one of the seeds inside a carob bean.

hundreds of years, people have learned how to grind the edges of a gemstone so that it sparkles as much as possible. Today, most gemstones are cut with special tools that have blades made of ground diamonds.

Creating the perfect combination of angled cuts, or **facets,** takes hours of patient work. After a gemstone is cut, light enters each facet and bounces around inside before shooting back out. The cut gives the gem its fiery brilliance.

Six of the most popular cutting patterns are the emerald cut, the round-brilliant cut, the pear-shaped brilliant cut, the cabochon, the table cut, and the heart-shaped brilliant cut.

Six of the most popular ways to cut a gem are shown below. From left to right, they are emerald, round brilliant, pear-shaped brilliant, cabochon, table, and heart-shaped brilliant.

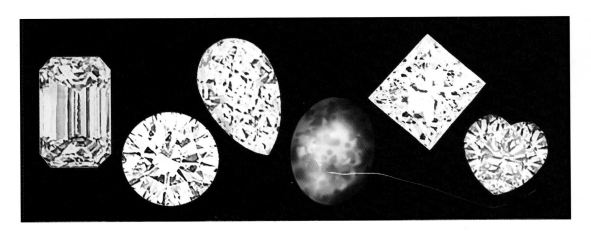

All about Diamonds

These rough diamonds are shown with a measuring instrument. They are of excellent quality and will be used in jewelry.

Diamond is one of the most important **minerals.** In many countries, diamond crystals are a symbol of everlasting love. That is why many people buy diamond engagement rings. Diamonds are also popular in other kinds of jewelry. The quality of a diamond **gem** depends on its color, clarity, size, and cut.

Diamond gems can be very expensive, so you might be surprised to hear that diamonds are not rare. In fact, more than ten tons of diamonds are mined every year. But only about 30 percent of all diamonds have the qualities needed to make beautiful gems. The rest are "bort"—diamonds used in industry. Because the carbon **atoms** that make up its structure are tightly packed, diamond is very hard. This makes it perfect for cutting other objects.

Most diamond forms in a kind of **igneous rock** called kimberlite. The rock is named after the town of Kimberley, South Africa, the site of the world's deepest diamond mine. While most of the world's diamonds come from South Africa, they can also be found in other parts of Africa and in Brazil, Australia, India, and Russia.

This diamond crystal is embedded in kimberlite, an igneous rock. Most diamonds are found in kimberlite that forms as **magma** cools deep below Earth's surface.

In 1905, Frederick Wells found a fist-sized diamond in South Africa. A few years later, thousands of diamonds were found scattered on the ground in a desert area in Namibia. Because the minerals had been exposed to many years of wear and tear, only the best diamonds had not been broken down into sand. As a result, nearly all of the diamonds found there could be used to make gems. These were the two most impressive diamond finds of all time.

WHAT A HISTORY!

Because diamonds are so valuable, the history of many of the most impressive ones has been carefully recorded. The famous Koh-i-noor diamond can be traced back more than 5,000 years. For centuries, it was passed from one Indian ruler to the next. But when the Muslims conquered the kingdom in 1526, the diamond became the property of the Mongol ruler Babur. It was stolen from his grandson and eventually returned to India. In 1849, British soldiers discovered the fiery gem and sent it to Queen Victoria as a gift. Today, the diamond still belongs to the British royal family.

Human-made Crystals

At one time, spinel (above) and garnet (below) were used to imitate rubies. Both crystals come in many different colors, depending on the **atoms** they contain.

Natural crystals form slowly over millions—or even billions—of years. That is why people have been searching for ways to imitate and make gemstones for at least 3,600 years. At first, people tried to pass off rock crystal as diamond. They used spinel and garnet to imitate ruby. Citrine, a kind of yellow quartz, was said to be topaz, and topaz was sold as yellow sapphire.

Although the equipment used to make artificial crystals is expensive, human-made crystals still cost 10 to 100 times less than the real thing. A 100-pound (45-kilogram) batch of cubic zirconia costs only a few dollars per carat. And while natural crystals are often flawed, artificial crystals are usually perfect. Also, they can be any size and shape.

The first real success in the effort to make artificial **gemstones** came in 1837, when a French scientist named Marc Gauder grew some artificial rubies in his lab. But he could make only flakes, not large crystals. In 1902, Antoine Vereuil, a scientist working at the Museum of Natural History in Paris, France, perfected a technique for making artificial ruby. It worked so well that we still use it today. A similar process is used to make artificial sapphire, spinel, emerald, and other gemstones.

In 1954, H. Tracy Hall, a scientist working at General Electric's Research Lab in Schenectady, New York, discovered a way to make artificial diamond that could be used for industrial purposes. He later said that when he realized his success, "My hands began to tremble; my heart beat rapidly; my knees weakened and no longer gave support. My eyes had caught the flashing light . . . and I knew that diamonds had finally been made by man." Today, Hall's process is used to make more than 44,000 pounds (nearly 20,000 kilograms) of artificial diamonds every year.

DID YOU KNOW?

Today's favorite diamond look-alike is cubic zirconia, which is made from superheated sand. Only an expert can tell the difference between a cubic zirconia and a diamond. A cubic zirconia crystal is the same color as a diamond and even sparkles like a diamond, but a diamond is harder and more durable.

How People Use Crystals

Of course, you already know that crystals of many **minerals** are cut to create the sparkling **gems** used in jewelry, religious objects, and pieces of art. But crystals are also used in many other ways.

We eat crystals of salt every day. It adds flavor to the food. Salt can also be used to preserve food for long periods of time and to melt the ice on roads in winter. Crystals of epsomite are the main ingredient in epsom salts. Dissolved in bath water, epsom salts clean cuts and reduce swelling. Quartz crystals are used to make the microchips that run our computers and keep our wristwatches running.

This microchip, smaller than an inch square, could not be made without quartz. Almost all microchips are made from silicon, the chief component of quartz.

When people look through a crystal of Iceland spar—a kind of calcite—they see two of everything. That's because when rays of light pass through this crystal, they separate and create a double image. This quality makes calcite crystals the perfect choice for building some kinds of microscopes.

About 70 percent of the diamond mined is not of high enough quality to be used as gems, but it is still useful. Because it is so hard, diamond is perfect for making dentists' drills, drill bits for oil wells, and special scalpels for very delicate surgeries. Diamond also carries sound and light waves well, so it is used in hearing aids, transmitters that carry telephone and television signals, and equipment used to locate fish and submarines in the ocean. Because diamond can tolerate extreme heat and cold, it has also been used to make the windows in some spacecraft and satellites.

Corundum is second only to diamond in hardness. Corundum crystals are used to grind and polish a variety of objects, including softer **gemstones.** They are also used to make emery paper and fingernail files.

This view through an electron microscope shows the diamond fragments on the tip of a dentist's drill. Diamond makes excellent drill material because it is the hardest mineral.

DID YOU KNOW?

The word "crystal" comes from a Greek term meaning "icy cold." The ancient Greeks believed that rock crystal, a kind of colorless quartz, was made of ice that had frozen so hard it would never thaw.

21

Where on Earth Are Crystals?

Crystals are found in the **minerals** in rocks all over the world. Within Earth's tallest mountains, below its widest plains, and underneath its ocean floor, lie a multitude of large and small crystals. Many of the largest and most prized crystals form in **igneous rock.** Igneous rock is brought to the surface as wind and water slowly break down the rock above it.

At Etta Mine near Keystone, South Dakota, miners found a pale-green crystal of spodumene that was as big as a house and weighed nearly 90 tons. But that's nothing compared to what workers discovered near Karrelia, Russia. The giant feldspar crystals found there weighed thousands of tons each.

This rare yellow sapphire was discovered in Sri Lanka. In Sri Lanka, sapphire and other gemstones are often found among sandy **sediment** in rivers and streams.

22

Sri Lanka, a tiny island country off the southeast tip of India, is sometimes called **Gem** Island. It has rich deposits of alexandrite, ruby, sapphire, topaz, garnet, spinel, and tourmaline. While some of the **gemstones** are mined, many can be found among pebbles **eroded** from larger rocks by heavy rains.

A large area of granite in northeast Brazil is also rich in gemstones. As the area was folded and uplifted by forces deep within Earth, the rock was brought to the surface. As heavy rains in the region slowly break down the granite, huge piles of gravel containing beautiful crystals of topaz, diamond, emerald, aquamarine, and tourmaline are left behind.

Emerald is a form of a colorless mineral called beryl. Just a few **atoms** of chromium give emerald its brilliant green color.

WHAT A DISCOVERY!

Some of the most valuable sapphires are mined from rock at Yogo Gulch in Montana's Little Belt Mountains. The gemstones were discovered in the late 1800s by a gold prospector named Jack Hoover. During a hailstorm, Hoover took shelter under a ledge. To pass the time, he scraped away some of the rock and later examined it to see if it contained any gold. The rock contained a little gold along with some small blue crystals. He sent the blue stones to an old girlfriend who lived in Maine. When she wrote to thank him for "the sapphires," Hoover realized that he had found something more valuable than gold, and opened a mine.

Crystal Powers

Crystals have fascinated people for thousands of years. The ancient Greeks and Romans thought fortune-tellers could see future events in crystal balls made of quartz. Some people believed that a diamond increased a person's strength, a peridot gave a person dignity, and an opal brought love and hope.

In some cultures, rubies symbolized power and romance. Others claimed that the brilliant red stone could cure diseases of the liver or spleen. Some people said the sapphire made a foolish person wise, but Roman Catholic priests often wore sapphire rings to symbolize their purity. Many soldiers were convinced that amethyst would keep them safe during battles and garnets would heal their wounds more quickly.

Sailors in some parts of the world believed that aquamarine brought them good luck at sea. Long ago, Native Americans belonging to the Navajo

In ancient times, some people placed emeralds under their tongues. They believed this would give them the power to predict the future.

DID YOU KNOW?

When ancient Egyptians mummified a ruler, they often placed an emerald in the person's throat. They believed that the gem would keep the person strong in the underworld.

tribe would throw turquoise into the river and say a prayer when they wanted rain.

Some people still believe that crystals have special powers. At Crystal Academy in Taos, New Mexico, students learn the art of crystal healing. When a person's body absorbs energy from the crystals, he or she supposedly heals more quickly.

For almost 2,000 years, people have called certain objects "birthstones," but people did not begin to wear birthstones as jewelry until the 1700s. Most of the birthstones are crystals, but a few are not. A pearl is not a crystal. It is made by a living animal—the oyster. An opal is sometimes called a **"gem,"** but it is made of tiny ball-shaped grains, not crystals. Turquoise is actually a rock made of many **minerals.**

The Greek word "amethystos" can mean "not drunken." The ancient Greeks believed that amethyst could cure drunkenness, so they often carved wine glasses from large amethyst crystals.

BIRTHSTONES BY MONTH

MONTH	BIRTHSTONE
January	Garnet
February	Amethyst
March	Aquamarine
April	Diamond
May	Emerald
June	Pearl
July	Ruby
August	Peridot
September	Sapphire
October	Opal
November	Topaz
December	Turquoise

Crystal Gallery

Most of the crystals that make up **minerals** are so small that you need a microscope to see them. But when crystals have enough space and time, they can grow quite large and be incredibly beautiful. Some of the most dazzling crystals are on display at museums around the world.

Topaz is a semiprecious **gem** that is usually golden brown, but it may also be colorless, pink, or pale blue. Stunning topaz crystals have been found in Russia and Brazil. The Brazilian Princess, the second largest topaz in the world, weighs 10 pounds (4.5 kilograms) and is the size of a car's headlight. During a two-year process, it was cut from a 26-pound (11.8-kilogram) **gemstone.**

Topaz crystals can be yellow, red, blue, green, or colorless. Yellow orange topaz gemstones are often used to make jewelry.

Most diamond is colorless, but the Hope diamond is a deep blue color. The diamond's color comes from a little bit of boron mixed in with the carbon **atoms.** At one time, people believed that this magnificent jewel brought bad luck to its owner.

The Hope diamond was found in India. Many impressive diamonds have also been found in South Africa. Today, the Hope diamond is on display at the Smithsonian Institution in Washington, D.C.

A **geode** is a round mass of rock that has a hollow cavity lined with large crystals. Most geodes contain crystals of the minerals quartz or calcite. A **nodule** is a round mass of rock completely filled with small crystals of agate, jasper, or chalcedony.

Both geodes and nodules are most often found within basalt, a kind of **igneous rock** that formed quickly as lava cooled. They may begin as large air bubbles in the lava or as animal burrows, tree roots, or mud balls swept up by the lava. Over time, the outside of the ball-shaped mass hardens, and water and dissolved minerals are trapped inside. As the water escapes, the atoms arrange themselves into repeating units. As more and more atoms join together, crystals begin to grow.

DID YOU KNOW?

Some minerals can have different kinds of crystals depending on how quickly they cool. Agate (above), jasper, chalcedony, amethyst, smoky quartz, and citrine are all forms of quartz. Crystals of agate, jasper, and chalcedony form quickly and are small. Amethyst, smoky quartz, and citrine have larger crystals because they cool more slowly.

A Closer Look at Crystals

A jewelry store is a good place to find crystals like these rubies and diamonds. You are not likely to find them in nature.

Now that you know all about the crystals that make up **minerals,** you may want to get a closer look at some. One of the best places to start is a local jewelry store. You will be able to see many beautiful **gems,** including diamonds, sapphires, rubies, amethysts, and peridots.

If you'd like to see some lovely crystals of minerals that are not durable enough to wear as jewelry, visit a natural history museum or attend a mineral show in your area. The people selling the minerals won't mind if you look at their samples, but don't touch them unless you intend to buy them.

You could even try hunting for large, beautiful crystals near your home. You probably won't find diamonds or emeralds, but you should be able to spot some quartz crystals. Quartz is the most common mineral on Earth's surface, and you can see quartz crystals in many rocks. If you decide to hunt for crystals outdoors, you will need to learn a few rules. You may also need to gather together some equipment.

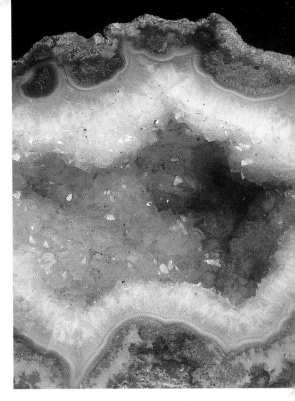

The **geode** is Iowa's official state rock, but can also be found in many other places. The layers of crystals inside a geode are formed when minerals in the rock cavity dissolve in water.

WHAT YOU NEED

- Hiking boots
- A map and compass
- A pick and rock hammer to collect samples
- Safety glasses to keep rock and mineral chips out of your eyes
- A small paintbrush to remove dirt and extra rock and mineral chips from samples
- A camera to take photographs of rock and mineral formations
- A hand lens to get an up-close look at crystals
- A notebook for recording when and where you find something interesting
- A field guide to rocks and minerals

WHAT YOU NEED TO KNOW

- Never look for crystals on your own. Go with a group that includes an adult.
- Know how to read a map and use a compass.
- Always get a landowner's permission before walking on private property. If you find some rocks with interesting crystals, ask if you may take them home.
- Before removing samples from public land, make sure collecting is allowed. Many natural rock formations are protected by law.
- Respect nature. Do not disturb living things, and do not litter.

Glossary

atom: smallest unit of an element that still has all the properties of the element

core: center of Earth. The inner core is solid, and the outer core is liquid.

crust: outer layer of Earth

crystallographer: scientist who studies crystals

erode: to slowly wear away rock over time by the action of wind, water, or glaciers

evaporate: to change from a liquid to a gas

face: smooth, flat side of a crystal

facet: angled cut a gem cutter makes to bring out a gem's beauty

gem: beautiful mineral that has been cut and polished

gemstone: beautiful mineral that may be worn as jewelry

geode: round mass of rock that has a hollow cavity lined with large crystals

igneous rock: kind of rock that forms when magma from Earth's mantle cools and hardens

magma: hot, soft rock that makes up Earth's mantle. When magma spills out onto Earth's surface, it is called lava.

mantle: layer of Earth between the crust and outer core. It is made of soft rock called magma.

mineral: natural solid material with a specific chemical makeup and structure. Most minerals have a crystal structure.

nodule: round mass of rock completely filled with small crystals

sediment: mud, clay, or bits of rock picked up by rivers and streams and dumped in the ocean

twinning: one crystal growing against or through another crystal

volcano: crack in Earth's surface that extends into the mantle, and from which comes melted rock

weathering: breaking down of rock by plant roots or by repeated freezing and thawing

To Find Out More

BOOKS

Blobaum, Cindy. *Geology Rocks!: 50 Hands-On Activities to Explore the Earth.* Charlotte, VT: Williamson, 1999.

Pellant, Chris. *Collecting Gems & Minerals: Hold the Treasures of the Earth in the Palm of Your Hand.* New York: Sterling, 1998.

Ricciuti, Edward, and Margaret W. Carruthers. *National Audubon Society First Field Guide to Rocks and Minerals.* New York: Scholastic, 1998.

Staedter, Tracy. *Rocks and Minerals.* Pleasantville, NY: Reader's Digest, 1999.

Stangle, Jean. *Crystals and Crystal Gardens You Can Grow.* New York: Franklin Watts, 1990.

Symes, R.F. *Crystals and Gems.* New York: Dorling Kindersley, 2000.

ORGANIZATIONS

Geological Survey of Canada
601 Booth Street
Ottawa, Ontario
KIA 0E8
613/995-3084

U.S. Geological Survey (USGS)
507 National Center
12201 Sunrise Valley Drive
Reston, VA 22092
703/648-4748

Index